The Wooly What's-It

This story shows that dealing with big problems is sometimes easier than we think.

Story by:
Ken Forsse

Illustrated by:
David High
Russell Hicks
Rennie Rau
Theresa Mazurek

WORLDS OF WONDER™

Grubby™ Newton Gimmick™ Princess Aruzia™ Leota™ Wooly What's-It™ Prince Arin™ Fobs™

We were near the Wooly What's-It's house.

Page 1

What is a Wooly What's-It?

Wooly, this is a very good dinner.

The wind was blowing so hard that it was difficult to tie down the airship.

Wooly, how can we ever repay you for saving the school tree?

It was a few days later that
we had a visit from Wooly.

Let's call it history.

Those big words shouldn't be scaring me.

The next time we went by the school tree, the Wooly What's-It was there.